Praise for **An**

Hannah Bonner's *Another Woman* is a meditation on the body, love and desire. The speaker asks, "When did I first define solitude as standing adjacent to objects without touching?" The poems provide answers in their lush and elegant language from the natural world to the bedroom, each season's slip falling to the naked floor. What is ruin to the already ruined, the claimed female body? To be the "other woman" is to be another woman "walking into the world with her palms open, accepting nothing but the fire." *Another Woman* will leave you breathless, "close to breaking."

—DIANNELY ANTIGUA, author of *Ugly Music* and *Good Monster*

A book of eros and "wild risk," Hannah Bonner's spellbinding debut, *Another Woman,* conjures "a water so febrile it is almost fire." In the aftermath of the end of a love affair, Bonner's speaker wonders tenderly about "every startled animal" and what it means to be a woman in the world when carnality gives way to grief. The speaker in her fever dream takes us deeper into her desire: a dizzying phantasmagory where stars are feet flung out of windows as the "sun kicks its heels" over the empty storefronts and fields of Arkansas. I am grateful for Bonner's fiercely intimate lyrics of womanhood, sexuality, loss, relief, and survival. *Another Woman* is hauntingly mesmerizing with poems of searing beauty, stellar power, and lyrical grace.

—CARLIE HOFFMAN, author of *This Alaska* and *When There Was Light*

I've been waiting for Hannah Bonner's debut book, *Another Woman,* for years, and it does not disappoint. A poet of the loud in the quiet, Bonner's poems are beautiful and exacting, and they don't shy away from penetrating self-reflection. I admire Bonner's bravery on the page; in a poem of parting, entitled, "Triumph," the poet writes, "Sometimes I am all of it: / sound, beauty, hunger." *Another Woman* explores all the others we inhabit in trying to become who we are, moving ultimately to a place of wonder—and love—for the self.

—LYNN MELNICK, author of *I've Had to Think Up a Way to Survive: On Trauma, Persistence, and Dolly Parton*

With her exquisitely sensual and razor-sharp debut collection *Another Woman*, Hannah Bonner has written "another kind of body." Pulse, gasp, tangle, flare—Bonner does not hesitate to say Yes again and again—to the shimmering natural world, to the past and present, to the body's orchard, to desire for its own sake. Invoking other women from Dido to Mary, Bonner's magnetic poems alchemize loss into love and offer new light to past lives. These poems hang on the "delicate thread between tenderness and terror," exploding judgments, expectations, and the familiar boundaries of a self. With a touch of fire that calls to mind Jean Valentine or Saskia Hamilton, these poems quicken and ache, hunger and heal, blossom and bark. The broken heart has never made such a startling garden. The moment I finished *Another Woman* I immediately began again, never wanting to finish.

—ELIZABETH METZGER, author of *Lying In* and *The Spirit Papers*

In this brutal, astounding collection, Bonner casts "relief across a blameless ground" like seeds begging for growth. In verse that punctures with sparse, aching specificity, Bonner writes with the fervor of a beast under threat: attentive, bare-toothed, unyielding. Like the quaking aftermath of a good fuck, these poems hum an ecstatically offbeat song I never want to be rid of. This is a debut so violent in its beauty, one can't help but tremble, open-mouthed like prey, before it.

—SPENCER WILLIAMS, author of *TRANZ*

ANOTHER WOMAN

Hannah Bonner

ANOTHER WOMAN

Hannah Bonner

ISBN 978-1-958094-54-9

POETRY

BOOK DESIGN ❦ EK Larken
COVER DESIGN ❦ Davin Malasarn
COVER ART ❦ Carl Elsaesser
AUTHOR PHOTO ❦ Julia Anna Morrison

EastOver Press encourages the use of our publications
in educational settings. For questions about
educational discounts, contact us online:
www.EastOverPress.com or info@EastOverPress.com.

PUBLISHED IN THE UNITED STATES OF AMERICA BY

EASTOVER PRESS
Rochester, Massachusetts
www.EastOverPress.com

Rumi says, out beyond ideas
of doing good and evil
there is a field

I'll meet you there

— FRANZ WRIGHT

for Anna, Hannah Leigh, and Isabella, always

CONTENTS

13 *FOREWORD by Louisa Hall*

17 Before the First

21 Marriage
22 Fireflies in July
23 Black Mountain, Highway 9
24 Disclosures
25 Trance
26 Among the Nouns at the Apocalypse
27 Inventory of Shimmers
28 Ruin
29 Waking Without You
30 Triumph
31 From Lot's Wife
32 Summer Solstice

35 In Kind
36 Instructions for Finishing
37 I Was a Liar
38 The Year I Was Born
39 Time Makes Me Human
40 Somewhere Else
41 From Dido
42 From Mary
43 Once You've Left
44 And when he told her it was truly over this time

47   The Ascetic

48   Pelt

49   Obituaries

50   Night, Memory

51   The Prize

52   In Spite Of

53   Sun in January, Three Months Since You've Left

54   In Time

55   Still Life with Citrus in February

56   To the Bone

59   Untitled

60   This Morning

61   A Passing

62   Lethe

63   Cosmogony

64   Final Hours

65   Another Woman

66   Rupture

67   My Body is Not Your Politics

68   Remember This

69   Another Ending for Aphrodite

70   Addendum

73   Pink Light

75   References

76   Acknowledgments

78   Thanks

81   About the Author

FOREWORD

One of my favorite discoveries this year has been Hannah Bonner's first book of poems, *Another Woman*. These poems are taut, bristling with verbs, so compressed they feel ready to spring off the page. They are playful and furious at once; elegiac and joyful. As the title suggests, there is nothing single or simple here. These are not poems about what it is to be a woman, alone: they are about what it is to be the other woman, outside a marriage; just another, statistical woman; one of the many women we become over the course of our lives; "a woman / anyone would recognize." It's almost choral, an inventory of female voices, including poems narrated by Delilah, by Lot's wife, by Mary, by Dido, and poems that incorporate the voices of Linda Kasbian, Karen Carpenter, and Simone Weil.

In its range, in its definition of womanhood as multiple and multiplying, it is vast, and yet each poem is whittled down to the bone. Whole lines are often pared to two words, stanzas to a single line, poems to a single stanza, as in this one, "From Mary":

> It is October. Everything is overturning.
> The field crackles. God tells me: the whole
> world is burning. I empty my pockets:
> three nails. I empty the table of all
> I have not eaten — carp bones,
> black dirt: aleatory, alarming.
> I light a match. Am inflamed, immediately.
> I put my ear to the earth, an organ humming —
> here, here it sings to me, insisting on its presence.
> The field becomes a votive. I shed my dress

like chaff. I'll figure this out or I won't:
Implacable, illusory, white as a receipt.

One line less than a sonnet, this is a poem about what we remove, what we empty, what we shed in the effort to figure out our place in the violent scheme of things as they currently exist. Reading it, as with others in this collection, I was tempted to think that these poems, tightened to the smallest versions of themselves, might represent the kinds of violence we have so often done to ourselves, in lieu of expressing our anger. But there is also an insistence here. "Here, here," the earth sings, and the poem also speaks in insistent, alliterative pairs: "aleatory, alarming,'" "inflamed, immediately," "implacable, illusory." This is a poem about what we don't eat, and yet it fills up our mouths with language: the crunch of "October," "crackles," "pockets"; "carp bones" and "black dirt." Each hard ending forces us to pause, to feel our tongues and our teeth. The page around it may be white as a receipt, but the space of the poem is thick with words, and impossible to read gently. It may be pared down, but it is pared to an edge we feel, an edge that is turned outward as well.

These poems are about women who experience pain and violence; but, especially as the book progresses toward its ending, they are also about women who escape, who find second and third iterations in which they use language to cut themselves free.

"I am the rupture / outracing the animal," Bonner writes. "I am the blue torrent / arrowing through earth."

These poems arrow and torrent, they rupture and outrace. The book gathers all this sharp-edged energy, and it feels like a triumph to read it.

—Louisa Hall
Associate Professor of Creative Writing at the University of Iowa,
author of the critically acclaimed novels *Reproduction, Trinity,* and *Speak*

ANOTHER WOMAN

Before the First

I am walking to you.

A thrash of moonlight,
its quiet kick.

Careful. Any day now.

The heart goes
out.

Where, you might ask?
Yes.

Marriage

The sun floats through me
like a young bride in a coffin.

Dust up the dirt road,
and all the way back down.

Fireflies in July

It's like a breath
breaching a dream —
a surge of stars cellular through grasses,
erotic as the pulse of skin before skin.
Like you looking at me,
the whole night turns over.
Rising, portent,
barely a glance,
barely green.

Black Mountain, Highway 9

Rhododendron click their curled leaves together
in the spangled shadows, a staccato of sound.

The August spider with a pale green belly
shifts on my wrist, going his tangled way.

From an old campfire, ashes stir themselves into air,
and a cardinal whistles through the clearing

like a painted red fan. When you rise from the water,
loose sand clinging to your calves, the amber current

rushing past the quiet, silver stones, you flare against the dark
like my heart, quickened to a melt.

All evening you dive and rise, all evening your swimming,
all that I see or would ever wish to see. Honey-streaked. Foaming.

Disclosures

In that
which is half lit,
like the white
peaches at dusk, still
cupping the heat
of the afternoon,
of August,
I am able to recognize
nothing more
than the outline
of my own figure,
and his,
the initial blues
of evening.

Seeing things
fully clothed —
the orchard winged
in green, wondering
when that branch
will bend, what could
possibly fill —

petals
closed, only to open,
like the shirt,
now discarded — another
kind of sheath
before the last light's
disclosure — another kind
of body, flower
twisting into fruit.

Trance

Finger in my mouth,
he goes quiet like a dream

in the dead of summer,
his eyes dark as iris

at Old Man's Creek.
Silent as a somnambulist

in the green gutted night, steady
and depthless as the river's pulse.

A water so febrile it is almost fire.
Our hunger is never enough.

Among the Nouns at the Apocalypse

Starlight and empty sidewalks, closed storefronts
       and cicadas, when did I first define solitude

as standing adjacent to objects
       without touching?

The streetlamps sputter Luna moths akimbo,
       a frantic arousal, their rinse of wings.

If no one arrives, I'll stay anyways,
       among the nouns, and their qualifiers,

breathing into my fragrant
       hands. In a clemency of wild air

my body bristles like an orchard cast in color,
       cleft through with want.

Inventory of Shimmers

This could be any place:
endless expanses
of grasses amidst the golden rod
that articulate a field.

Or, to put it more precisely,
articulate the field visible,
a sign unto itself.
I walk the pathway

past the flora so furtive
and folded they demand a kind
of attention like the lamentation
before a burning — and the torch of the moon

swarms the surface both above,
and below, bright.
Tell me to hope,
I won't believe you.

Tell me to wait like a woman
anyone would recognize,
walking into the world with her palms open,
accepting nothing but the fire.

Ruin

Pinned to the white wall
the ruched dress pulses
like gills, an open

throat widely
tonguing,
a muscle so worn

you could never color it
coral, but *ash*, *animal*:
a body that multiplies itself

like spores, like sickness.
Look how the tacks tear
the skin: how delicate the thread

between tenderness and terror,
how black the cords that shape the hem
like shoreline without moonlight.

Waking Without You

Another call and message left
while I stand at the stove,

waiting for the coffee, pretending
not to hear. Outside the window

a buck stands in the field, head cocked
like a telephone, all rapture and ear:

when I see him, the antlers
coming through harvest

that stretches
across the plain, it is not

unlike your hand
on my body when it gathered

another yield in the dark —
more like the locust, than the buck,

at the wheat's throat, more
whittling it open, then coming

through — noise
low in the flesh,

in the field,
more waiting

for that ache
and after, echo

of the ache
in air.

Triumph

You say, *you don't get to make me*
the enemy any longer.

Your mouth on my mouth
after the final

exclamation of anger.
In present tense, the echo

deepens, agape,
between us.

Sometimes the sound we make
devours us.

Sometimes the sound we make
is beautiful.

Sometimes I am all of it:
sound, beauty, hunger.

From Lot's Wife

I stopped speaking because God
was already in my ear. I rolled up

my tongue like a rug I couldn't
find a room for. I ate salt, incessantly.

No one will tell me how to be forgiven.

I don't pray often, but when I do
its cadence is sweetness. My heart

whips through me: ionized,
electric, a pillar of impatience. They say

Zoar is where paternity short circuits
and the air immolates us all asunder.

The angels flare: this I know:
I had so many warnings.

Summer Solstice

Caravan of moonlight rushing through me
like the urgency of deer.
We insist until we remember
the brightness in the dark.

In Kind

I became the other woman
gradually, then suddenly.

We shared
the same name. Her

hair was dark like my hair.
She spoke

in a speaking voice
like I do.

When she clasped her hands, it was I
who was touched.

Sometimes she calls to me,
and I answer in kind.

Split infinity
and the violet flame

of knowledge.
The scream lives in the mirror.

Woman woman woman

Instructions for Finishing

We quickened in the open air
of your apartment where I uttered

your name, reddish
as an asterism of stars. *I love you I love*

you we insisted, turning under
each other's body,

teeth furred from a mouthful
of vintage: burning skin

burgundy, bestiary.
Sometimes it seems

the ineffable is the only evidence
I was here,

braced beneath you,
betrayal a forked and tautological

dream. I won't repair
your marriage I almost ruined.

I won't hate myself more than necessary.

Before the paradise of feeling,
this brutal, risen heaven.

Not yet I told you to tell me when I was close
to breaking.

I Was a Liar

from Delilah

It was your hair I wanted.
The heft of it.
Its rain beating down upon me
until I shut my eyes,
lids seamed with wet and glare.
The betrayal,
that came later —
an animal inside me bleating.
I muzzled the noise.
I smothered the silence.
My wild risk, my white lie:
God was with you —
I always knew that —
even when they strung you
up like a star,
blind and shorn.
You fevered through me,
those nights you hung there,
a split flesh, spasmodic,
forking.

The Year I Was Born

Prozac went on the market. My grandfather,
the psychiatrist, wrote my grandmother a prescription.
Mary Gaitskill published *Bad Behavior* and S&M
shipped to suburbia. Thirty years later I only masturbate
to fantasies of control and measured tenderness.
"I don't want to hurt you," you tell me. You do,
just on a smaller scale, as I intended. The year I was born
people wore scrunchies without irony, or shame. It was a leap
year. My father was the age I am now, my mother:
five years younger. People still drank milk
and sunbathed and smoked, ardently. Women teased
their hair. Bermuda was a vacation destination *because some people*
always have to have something in the fire. Coke was just barely
out of vogue. You could say everyone was having the time
of their lives — you could say that. I would later run
away from every nice boy so fast I'm still running to get
back to where I began. I flirt often, but forget — am I
terrified? Does my mouth move like an animal, all synapse
and gristle? I am learning to enunciate even with your cock
crammed in my face, so goddamn sure you're like the sky
opening: clear, chorus. I took so many sleeping pills the year
of the election. You know which one I'm talking about:
the year I lost my profitability and prosody, with plenty of warning.
In book club we collectively admit we've never read Hegel, but now
seems as good a time as any. We set our vulnerability on ice,
on velvet. We have never been so bold in our address,
so lacking in capital. The year I was born Lis Rhodes told me:
The arrangement of facts sprang easily into fiction.
There's no spring anymore, or past tense, or fact.
I am rooting down in the fallacy of my whole fucking life.

Times Makes Me Human

Quiet gasp of stars
like feet flung out a window —
supplicate me,
my only surviving light.

Somewhere Else

Beer bottles slick my truck bed
in their stranglehold as I idle
by water in Arkansas.

Bats test the thinning air
with their velvet tongues.
The sun kicks its heels

like a federation,
like a burning house with all the lights on.
From a squint I can see the day

shrug off its slip. Somewhere else,
where I should be,
there's no dinner wrapped in cellophane,

no glass of milk bright white in the dark room,
no bed low as a lake for me to dip in,
private and damp with your dreams,

your odors.
The path breathes out its lung
of dust, and I am done for.

All my life I've been licked and loping:
neck bent like a faucet,
angling to be halfway good.

From Dido

It wasn't my dress that went first,
slightly damp with the sweat of my labor,
but my hair — the flames a branching
antler, a scorching crown. The scent
of smoke released a panic,
but I was steady and fixed as your destination.
When you looked back at the black
cloud of Carthage, you still did not
see me — my throat upturned
to a sky that precedes air and song. Don't tell me
this knots your heart of oak. Don't follow
me into the dim hallways of Erebus, trembling
like a thistle with the Fates' excuses. I am sifting
like a spate of stars, a cooling calm, a queen,
a woman, a warning.

From Mary

It is October. Everything is overturning.
The field crackles. God tells me: *the whole
world is burning.* I empty my pockets:
three nails. I empty the table of all
I have not eaten — carp bones,
black dirt: aleatory, alarming.
I light a match. Am inflamed, immediately.
I put my ear to the earth, an organ humming —
here, here it sings to me, insisting on its presence.
The field becomes a votive. I shed my dress
like chaff. I'll figure this out or I won't:
implacable, illusory, white as a receipt.

Once You've Left

October light pierces possibility
right out of the air. Tree trunks

unmoved as a haunting. Birds darken
with worry in a crushing

autumn wind, and a barge cleaves
the Mississippi, smooth as repetition

with no difference. Everything hushes
before the worst of it —

how a doctor tells you to relax
before administering pain.

Keep my heart, you can't cure it. Tonight,
I'll lie down with the ear of another.

At every hour
the river wheels and eddies.

Promise me
the song always comes back.

And when he told her it was truly over this time

he looked at her like November light flung
long across a porch.

.

The Ascetic

When you left me, I walked for miles every night
through farmland and fields.

I could hear the animals all around me.
It was like walking inside a nightmare:

the tumult of stars overhead radiant
and fanged.

When I put salt on my windowsill,
deer licked it dry.

When the air around me roiled,
I pushed past its cooling currents

down the hill to the deep lake.
That winter, any man I welcomed loved

less than I loved.
You could smell my desperation

like livestock in the factory a few miles from town.
I kept rocks in my boots daily to remind myself

the pain was real. I promise you: when I knelt,
it was not for penance, but for this, this glory.

Even now I couldn't tell you the color of the dark
when I was just a girl.

Pelt

Bright as deer —
a shaft of skin,
sacrament,
strange country
you
who is missing

Obituaries

Linda Kasbian said she and the women
did *anything and everything* for Charlie

without refusal.
They bit their wrists

only occasionally
to remember

they were alive.
Karen Carpenter sang

angels, dust, moonlight,
you — tremulous in the auditorium.

Simone Weil sucked
the pus of lepers

to come
closer to God.

Everything I've archived exists
in the silver exhaustion of endings.

The teeth so white in the photograph,
like pearls, plucked

from a silk lined leatherette,
at the margins of language.

Night, Memory

There is never just one deer.
The forest clicks bare branches

under a bristling moon.
The field strobes in slow motion,

the sky clean and clear
as a bloodletting.

I am here again
without the bottle or the blade,

my good hands empty,
doing nothing they are asked.

In the blue bedroom of my childhood
my uncle calls me by my given name.

Shivering in the doorway,
I am the bare one

braced like a star, or girl.

The damp field mutes the gallop
of every startled animal.

There is never just one
deer in the middle of the night.

The Prize

When I became a single woman,
the men swarmed all around me.

It seemed the more I was,
the more they multiplied

with their prophecies,
and their payments, and their wagging,

tepid tongues.
Their attention, it angered me.

How they told me not to
worry. How they told me

they'd be back.
The worst ones

I let do whatever they wanted.
My body — a glass

or liquid —
submitting to their heat.

(I have loved
three men in my life.

I have held one
up to the light.)

In Spite Of

and when you told me you loved
your wife

it didn't matter

and when you sent for me
in another state

it didn't matter

and when you told me to leave
the next morning

it didn't matter

and when you said you wouldn't touch me
(and you touched me)

it didn't matter

and when I wept, swore,
had other men (again and again)

it didn't matter

and when I finally made haste
like a heroine

it didn't matter

I did it all
(and then some)

to speak achingly
and to live.

Sun in January, Three Months Since You've Left

I can hear ice
all around me
breathing

In Time

Better the *because of* —
bright utter.

Better the leaving,
had before.

Better the lover,
than the other.

Better the gasp, a last
grasp, a postlude.

Better the split
lighting up in glints,

better the breath, than the hint,
its aperture (its click),

his *never*
again. Then his *ok*.

Better the beginning,
which never ended,

its blue rooms,
passageways.

Still Life with Citrus in February

This morning I look at the wedding
ring I never wore, the lemons limning

the wooden bowl, furred
white from age and heat.

There is snow again. There is morning
again. There is the predictable

deer print tracking
the perimeter of the house.

Last year I let a love go,
then lost another.

What this is
it is, no matter

where you edge.

There is sun again.
There is luck again.

Relief across a blameless ground,
a bright light,

no longer begging.

To the Bone

Not the deer I dream of,
nor the melt's quick

and shallow stream.
Not the rush, the run, breaking

through meadow with moonlight —
the damp earth, the animal,

the trees. Not the blade on the bath
I walk away from,

skin parting air
like rain. Not the wet

want inside me which whispers
spring is coming,

cupped low and mulched at my ear.
Not the crocus, not the coming,

always already inside you.
Not the deer. Their pelts.

Their panting. No, not even
after — their clamor to the bone.

Untitled

I know I am safe
when I sense the deer.

Only I can
startle them.

This Morning

Wind devours me like a whole life
left open.
Space, allowance, stars —
everything I'll take.

A Passing

Even now, the extraordinary
silence of almost a year past — blue and pine.
The deep meadow presses down the dark
that can't come quick enough,
wheat grinds to its knees.
The moon's technical presence
does not disappoint tonight,
her usual rise and fall through horse
and yearning. And your voice — like those stars
made immutable by their very stillness —
a singular heat burning,
your absence again restored.

Lethe

In the predawn bluish milk
of forgetting, a bit more

green — and the dirt darker
where the leaves mulch over.

Every day a wilderness
my body can't contain.

Every day an other.
The clock ticks,

the sun salts air,
the light the light the light

Cosmogony

And yet
still — no part of the day

lasts long enough
to hold it.

Stone, fire,
then the carbon rings,

swallowing up, then spitting,
small spasms of a life.

Final Hours

I felt around in the dark
for you. The stars

like little notes we tack up
in order to survive.

It felt like midnight.
It felt like midlife.

All the clocks — cede me.
I am touching

risk (its stretching) —
OK, now its rim —

Another Woman

I wait for night
to turn over within me.

Then another woman
walks out of the space

where I have been.
Like pine

in an open window,
and the light there,

lengthening —
and the rain. The rain.

Its heaving. Its pulsing fold,
its blue.

Rupture

Rain splits soil
like a gasp of stallions

let out to pasture
in lightning.

They blot
the hill —

stippled mane,
twitch of tail,

blank face turning
towards me.

I carry a long-lost love pressed
deep within my skins,

wet and matted
as a meadow.

Second life,
grant me passage

from the glittering blackout
of time.

I am the rupture
outracing the animal.

I am the blue torrent
arrowing through earth.

My Body is Not Your Politics

On the bus, in the Laundromat,
in the classroom, on the stained

mattress, stuck in line for groceries,
pressed together, like petals

in a book, waiting for the sign "walk"
in green, my body is not your politics.

In the dark tunnel of the alleyway
building with the tumult

of a March wind, among the blue
fissures of the call light on the college campus,

between the arms of his embrace
mussing the ink on the page

of the last word in this sentence —
my body — as vast as the silence

stretched between the man and the woman
in the poem — my body — the spring sky, blown

clear of clouds, the small indentation
of last night's moon, still

present and virtuous — as my body,
my body filled with longing, longing

then relief, still churning, still declarative,
shaking like the Lilacs lining the street,

all blossom, blossom
and bark.

Remember This

I wake up this morning
and say, *yes.*

Rise to a tumult of finches
buffeted by wind

and say, *yes.*
Brew the bad coffee

with my own two hands
and say, *yes.*

Look at the oaks
fluted with mist, and the sun

piercing through them
and say, *yes. Yes.*

I don't consult a clock.
I will not rush anymore.

The white curtains ribbon
in the open window

with the violet streaks of rain.
Yes, this earthen color.

And the sound bearing down
upon me.

I touch myself. I love myself.
I am the garden of wonder.

Another Ending for Aphrodite

And when she promised she would
never give herself to another,
Hephaestus embraced her,
relieved, like a flame encircling the wick,

shuddering with air, and she rose
to meet his teeth, tongue,
and thigh. *Better to be alone*, she thought
afterwards, *than beholden to another.*

It is almost August now as she collects
olive branches in the dusk. No jewelry
in the hair, nothing but sun
on the nape. And each nail muddied

as an eel eye. Hephaestus is swimming
in the sea alone and does not call her to him.
It'll be better this way, she thinks, *no more
expectations.* She rearranges

the branches, drenched in the dust of the day.
Brushes insects off her arms. Whistles
with the thicket of murmurings
the whole length of the white road.

Addendum

When the landscape hushes over
(the sun so low I could eat it)
the tenor of cicadas and crickets darken
as the field pinkens gold.

No one on the path tonight,
past the subdivisions and backyards,
just the prairie that flushes
with wildflowers and beyond

that brightness, corn.
At vespers, I slow my steps
to savor the minutes
as shadows stretch forth,

beckoning like a hand. And I think,
alone I am witness to my wonder
full of luster at the fulcrum
of one space to the next.

Pink Light

At sunset I walk toward you,
across a harrowed field.

Pink light, winter solstice,
wait

for my second coming.
I swear

I'll do better next time,

give up
the past, and shame.

Once you said I opened
the space outside your body,

forever branching for, then through.
Again, I am at that juncture,

ascending earth, moon,
erotic.

Luminous you were made, and always
I am here.

REFERENCES

The lines "Tell me to hope, I won't believe you" in "Inventory of Shimmers" is a riff off a stanza in Louise Glück's "October": "Tell me this is the future, / I won't believe you. / Tell me I'm living, / I won't believe you."

The title "Inventory of Shimmers" is a phrase from Roland Barthes that Gregory J. Seigworth and Melissa Gregg unpack in their book *The Affect Theory Reader*.

"Ruin" was written in response to a piece of art by Maggie Jaszczak for *PromptPress*.

The line "people always have to have something in the fire" in "The Year I Was Born" is from a *New York Times* article "Vacation's Over, but the Mind Still Wanders" by Michael Decourcy Hinds, published on September 7, 1988.

ACKNOWLEDGMENTS

Thank you to the editors of the following publications, in which some of the poems in this book first appeared, occasionally in different iterations:

"This Morning" appeared in a 2021 limited letterpress zine from 508 Press.

A Room of Her Own Foundation ~ "My Body is Not Your Politics"

Bear Review ~ "Obituaries"

Cutleaf ~ "Once You've Left," "The Prize," "In Spite Of," and "Still Life with Citrus in February"

North Carolina Literary Review ~ "Another Ending for Aphrodite"

Pigeon Pages ~ "Somewhere Else"

PromptPress ~ "Ruin"

Rattle ~ "And when he told her it was truly over this time"

SAND ~ "In Time"

Schlag Magazine ~ "From Dido" and "I Was a Liar"

Small Orange ~ "Night, Memory"

The Carolina Quarterly ~ "Trance," "Lethe," and "Pink Light"

The Freeman ~ "Waking Without You"

The Hopkins Review ~ "In Kind"

The LaHave Review ~ "Pelt"

The Pinch Journal ~ "From Mary" and "From Lot's Wife"

The Southern Poetry Anthology, Volume VII: North Carolina ~ "Black Mountain, Highway 9" and "Disclosures"

The Vassar Review ~ "The Year I Was Born"

The West Review ~ "To the Bone"

TriQuarterly Review ~ "Among the Nouns at the Apocalypse"

Two Peach ~ "A Passing"

Volume Poetry ~ "Instructions for Finishing"

Washington Square Review ~ "Before the First"

West Trade Review ~ "The Ascetic"

THANKS

To Denton Loving and everyone at EastOver Press for this incredible opportunity.

To Diannely Antigua, Carlie Hoffman, Lynn Melnick, Elizabeth Metzger, and Spencer Williams for your generous blurbs. They are true gifts. I admire each and every one of you beyond measure.

To the Vermont Studio Center for affording me the time and space to work on this manuscript in 2017.

To my parents: none of this would be possible without your love. Thank you for inspiring me to be a writer.

To my first and most steadfast friend, my brother Willie, whose appetite for the outdoors is a constant source of inspiration.

To Pete Upham, my first poetry teacher — thank you for every assignment, every exercise, and every note. You taught me not just how to be a better poet but how to take myself seriously as a writer. That lesson was, and is, invaluable.

To Larry Kollath who nudged me towards poetry again when I thought I had lost all interest. You knew I was meant to be doing this. I miss you.

To those who read various iterations of this manuscript and offered invaluable feedback including Alisha Jeddeloh, Andrew David King, Nina Lohman, Catherine Pond, Cory Hutchinson-Reuss, William Rhodes, and Spencer Williams.

Special gratitude to Carl Elsaesser for permission to use a still from his stunning film *Home When You Return* (2021) for the cover — I remain endlessly grateful to be in an ongoing dialogue with your work.

To my NWP Workshop at the University of Iowa, in particular Sarah Adler, Rebecca Flowers, Mason Hamberlin, Sarah Khatry, and Cathryn Klusmeier. A special thanks to Dr. Sarah Minor, the most caring and careful reader (and essayist) I know.

To @poetryisnotaluxury on Instagram. We've never met, but I feel your love and support, fiercely.

To Matt, Stephen, and Aaron — so much of this was written while we lived together. Thank you for loving me unconditionally.

To Louisa Hall whose grace and guidance inspires me as both a woman and a writer. Thank you for your words. My own can't do justice other than to say our conversations have enriched my writing life beyond measure.

To the loves of my life — my favorite poet, Anna. You are such a source of strength and inspiration. Thank you for always reorienting me back to the fiercest facets of myself. You are a woman I seek to emulate.

Hannah Leigh who has been a loyal friend since the beginning and shows up year after year reassuring me: I am here, I love you, I am listening. If I can ever be a fraction of the person you are, I will have lived a good life. Your empathy, care, and capacity for growth is astounding. I love you dearly.

My sister, Isabella, who read every single poem in this manuscript multiple times and whose very existence makes this world worth living in. To paraphrase Ocean Vuong, with your birth it will be joy from now on. The gift is you.

ABOUT THE AUTHOR

HANNAH BONNER'S criticism has appeared in
Cleveland Review of Books, *Literary Hub*, the *Los
Angeles Review of Books*, *Senses of Cinema*, *The
Rumpus*, and *The Sewanee Review*, among oth-
ers. She is a 2023-2024 National Book Critics
Circle Emerging Critics Fellow and a graduate
of the University of Iowa's MFA in creative
nonfiction. Originally from Asheville, North
Carolina, she currently lives in Iowa.

Printed in the USA
CPSIA information can be obtained
at www.ICGtesting.com
CBHW062058020724
11053CB00003B/3